Contents

Maps: Languages p. 13, Geneva p. 21, Lake of Geneva p. 35, Lausanne-Centre p. 40, Switzerland p. 54–55.

How to use this guide
If time is short, look for items to visit which are printed in bold type, e.g. **Saint-Saphorin.** Those sights most highly recommended are not only given in bold type but also carry our traveller symbol, e.g. **Château de Chillon.**

The Region and the People

Unlike those intriguing Swiss bank accounts, the nation's visible marvels are numberless: peaks covered with eternal snow, deep green valleys, medieval castles and tidy villages. And don't forget the famous cheese, chocolate and clocks. Everything is squeezed into less than 16,000 square miles; two Switzerlands would fit neatly into Ireland.

Deep cultural currents converge at this landlocked linguistic crossroads. Three major European languages are offici-

ally used in Switzerland. Sixty-five percent of the people speak a species of German; 18 percent claim French as their mother tongue; and 12 percent (including immigrants from south of the border) speak Italian. A fourth language, Romansh, is proudly preserved by about one percent of the population, mostly in isolated eastern districts. Switzerland has so many official names—Schweiz, Suisse, Svizzera—that the coins and postage stamps identify it in Latin: Helvetia.

Valais village girls in festive finery scamper over the cobblestones; cycling through Jura farm country.

This book covers the French-speaking region, the western fourth of the country, known as Suisse Romande*. Here the heart inevitably leans toward Paris but the Swissness scarcely relents: Lausanne's Métro trains depart every 7½ minutes—by the second-hand!

French-speaking Switzerland has no single cultural or political capital. Its biggest city, Geneva, was the Rome of the Protestant world in the 16th century, but some other parts of Suisse Romande remain solidly Catholic. The linguistic and religious divergences among the Swiss usually balance out in peaceful coalitions and compromises.

Geneva's setting is superb—aristocratic houses and gardens astride the narrow tip of the biggest lake in the Alps. Over the years, the Lake of Geneva (the correct name is Lac Léman) has attracted a good deal of foreign talent: Byron, Gogol, Stravinsky, Nabokov, Charlie Chaplin. The lake also supplies inspiration to the likes of the Aga Khan and the Emir of Qatar... and ordinary tourists who don't require a palace to appreciate the reflections of the Alps in its deep, sparkling but changeable waters.

The principal port on this international lake (you can sail over to France for lunch!) is Lausanne, capital of the populous canton of Vaud and world headquarters of the Olympic games. Both Geneva and Lausanne have important cathedrals and universities. Other towns of the region have their own religious or intellectual traditions superimposed on enthralling scenery. Fribourg perches above a deep winding river. Neuchâtel sprawls along its own lake. Sion, in Valais, lives beneath a pair of surrealistic humped hills, themselves dwarfed by surrounding Alps.

Not everything is monumental or serious. At the eastern end of the Lake of Geneva, on the almost tropical shore known as the Vaud Riviera, flower-bedecked Montreux plays host to celebrated music festivals. Inland, in the tiny trim village of Gruyères, folklore and cheese make the world go round. And in almost any town you may stumble upon local seasonal festivals enlivened by authentic costumes, flowers and the blare of brass bands.

* The eastern and central regions of the country are covered in a companion Berlitz guide: SWITZERLAND: GERMAN-SPEAKING AREAS

Market day: the freshest flowers, crispest cabbages, sleekest leeks.

Fine ensemble of low-rise buildings grace the Right Bank of Geneva.

Unless you're addicted to museums and historic churches —with which the region is bountifully supplied—you'll probably spend most of your time outdoors in the deliciously pure air. The choice of activities, from lazy to strenuous and daring, couldn't be bigger. Climb a mountain or ride a horse. Ski (the year round!) or play tennis or golf. Swim or sail, water-ski or fish. Or stroll at your own pace through the verdant countryside.

Between energetic outbursts you can settle down in a park or café and watch the Swiss: athletic-looking women with overfed dogs, well-mannered children greeting you with a "*Bonjour, monsieur* (or *madame*)", neatly uniformed street-cleaners operating mechanical scrubbers which shine the pavements, less neatly uniformed citizen-soldiers lugging their automatic rifles off to a spell of training. Yes, strangely enough, neutral, peaceful Switzerland bristles with permanent preparations against any foreign attack— tanktraps, camouflaged bunkers, airstrips hidden in bucolic valleys with underground park-

ing for the jets, and an army reserve of every able-bodied male up to the age of 50.

The man in the street not only defends his country but takes a big part in running it. Swiss direct democracy puts more power in the hands of the individual citizen, the town and the canton (state) and less at the centre. Local initiatives propose new laws and popular referendums approve or reject them.

Although the French-speaking Swiss tend to take life more casually than their compatriots in German-speaking Zurich or Basel, pedestrians still wait interminably for the traffic light to change, rather than jay-walk across an empty street. Residents of Montreux receive an official seven-page illustrated booklet explaining how, where and when to dispose of rubbish. All this order and organization seems even more remarkable when you consider that nearly one out of every six inhabitants is a foreigner: a political exile, a "guest worker" or a tax-sensitive film star.

The Swiss standard of living is enviably high: per-capita income far exceeds that in the United States. Moreover, this prosperity has been attained with almost no conventional natural resources. It's Swiss ingenuity and perfectionism that makes the difference.

But industriousness, thrift and discretion don't interfere with good times. Even in Calvin's Geneva the nightclub patrons frolic far into the night. And by way of simple pleasures you can stop in any café and try the wine from just up the hill—unassuming as a mountaineer's hut. As for the food, local cooks rarely strive for gourmet productions, but they turn out home-style food you'll like. The quantity, though, is almost overwhelmingly generous. If Swiss cuisine consisted of nothing more elaborate than the cheese, it would still be a winner.

In all the bigger towns the shop windows are seductive: gold watches and jewellery, furs and fashions. If your budget keeps you outside looking in, you can still enjoy all the colour of a street market. Once or twice a week almost every town and village has an outdoor bazaar—freshly picked flowers, fruits and vegetables, home-made sausages and bread.

You may never want to leave this little, well-ordered world of scenic grandeur where hospitality, good food and drink are served up with admirable efficiency.

A Brief History

The story of Switzerland has a happy ending—liberty, peace and prosperity. But first came centuries of struggle against nature and hostile neighbours.

Cave-men inhabited Switzerland 10,000 years ago, picking berries, hunting reindeer and trying to elude the tusks of wandering mammoths. After another 5,000 years of development, neolithic settlers built stilt houses around Alpine lakes, grew grain and raised livestock.

During the second Iron Age, around 400 B.C., Celtic tribesmen arrived from the north with a more advanced culture. They were called Helvetians, and from them derives the original name of Switzerland, Helvetia.

Surrounded by hostile Germanic tribes, the Helvetians initiated a scorched-earth policy, burning their farms and houses and emigrating en masse across Gaul. But Roman legions, commanded by Julius Caesar, blocked their path in 58 B.C. The Helvetians, about whom Caesar wrote flattering reports, were forced to return home. Under Roman control the old Helvetian town of Aventia became Aventicum, administrative centre of Ro-

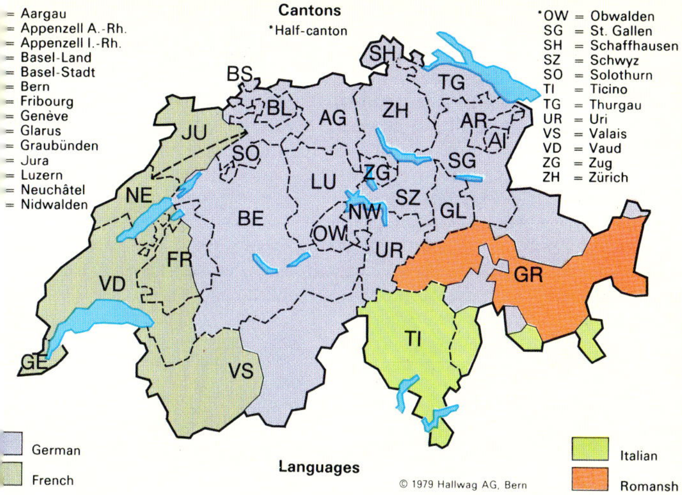
Cantons
*Half-canton
= Aargau
= Appenzell A.-Rh.
= Appenzell I.-Rh.
= Basel-Land
= Basel-Stadt
= Bern
= Fribourg
= Genève
= Glarus
= Graubünden
= Jura
= Luzern
= Neuchâtel
= Nidwalden
*OW = Obwalden
SG = St. Gallen
SH = Schaffhausen
SZ = Schwyz
SO = Solothurn
TI = Ticino
TG = Thurgau
UR = Uri
VS = Valais
VD = Vaud
ZG = Zug
ZH = Zürich
SH
BS
TG
BL
AG
ZH
AR
AI
JU
SO
SG
LU
ZG
NE
SZ
NW
GL
BE
OW
UR
FR
GR
VD
TI
GE
VS
German
French
Languages
© 1979 Hallwag AG, Bern
Italian
Romansh

man Switzerland. Imperial Aventicum, nearly 60 kilometres north-east of the Roman trading post of Lousonna (now Lausanne), is today's sleepy village of Avenches.

The Romans built international roads through Switzerland, bringing the latest technology and culture and, eventually, the new religion of Christianity. With the collapse of the Roman empire, the Burgundians moved into western Switzerland, while the east fell to the Alemanni, fierce Germanic tribesmen. This dividing line between the Burgundians and the Alemanni, along the Sarine River, still more or less forms the linguistic frontier between French-speaking and German-speaking Switzerland.

The Middle Ages

Switzerland was briefly united under Charlemagne's Holy Roman Empire in the 9th century, but all Europe soon splintered into feuding feudal city-states, dukedoms and family fiefs. By the middle of the 13th century, two powers predominated: the House of Savoy and the Habsburgs. In central Switzerland local resistance to the widening Habsburg power led to a mutual assistance pact in 1291 between the communities of Uri, Schwyz and Unterwald, which snowballed over the next century into a full-fledged confederation of eight cantons united against all foreign perils. This was the era of William Tell, who shot an apple from the head of his small son at 100 paces. Actually, discrepancies in the story of Tell, ace archer and foe of tyrannical overlords, prompt some critical historians to believe Switzerland's greatest hero was just a myth.

Nobody, though, doubts the courage and prowess of medieval Swiss soldiers. They impressed invaders so often that a new export trade began: Swiss troops hired out as mercenaries, sometimes on both sides of a war. The sight of these tough peasants with their heavy, deadly halberds was an important psychological weapon. Descendants of the halberdiers, in medieval finery,

Picture of defeat: with the Swiss in hot pursuit, Charles the Bold of Burgundy flees 1476 battlefront.

may still be seen on guard at the Vatican … the only Swiss warriors in foreign service today.

The best advertisement for Swiss military efficiency may have been Charles the Bold, the hard-hitting Duke of Burgundy. He lost two disastrous battles to the Swiss in 1476. At Grandson, on Lake Neuchâtel, Swiss troops routed the duke and his army; he is said to have decided to retreat when he heard the ghastly sound of a Swiss horn. Looking for revenge, the brave duke laid siege to the walled town of Morat, about 40 kilometres away as the arrow flies. A vast Swiss relief column came to the rescue of the Morat garrison, thrashing the Burgundians and pursuing them without mercy. It was a notable massacre. The duke's fortunes continued to decline and he was killed the following year in the battle of Nancy. The Swiss remember Grandson and Morat with unconcealed pride.

Overcoming Setbacks

The seemingly invincible Swiss split forces (half of them settled with François Ier and returned home) and met defeat in 1515, at the hands of the French, in the battle of Marignano (Italy). One of the generals on the French side chivalrously described it as the battle of giants, but kind words couldn't change the verdict. Switzerland had to lick its wounds and take stock of its position as a small country surrounded by powerful, squabbling neighbours. The solution was neutrality—a policy as enduringly Swiss as the mountains.

During the 16th century the chronic tensions within Europe were drastically heightened by the Protestant Reformation. In 1522, five years after Martin Luther hammered home his 95 **15** theses in Germany, a Swiss curate, Ulrich Zwingli of Zurich, challenged the pope's authority. Protestantism spread more slowly in the French-speaking region, but by 1542 the French reformer John Calvin had established a severe Protestant theocracy in Geneva. And the Bernese occupied the canton of Vaud and brought the Reformation with them. Some blood was spilled on both sides in the Reformation and Counter-Reformation.

But the Swiss stayed on the sidelines of Europe's great religious and political struggle, the Thirty Years' War. Swiss Catholics and Protestants tried to live together behind the shield of neutrality, meanwhile prospering by supplying both warring sides. When peace finally came to Europe with the treaty of Westphalia (1648), the independence of the sovereign state of Switzerland was at last universally acknowledged.

The after-shock of the French Revolution (1789) reverberated across all of Europe, not least in Switzerland. After occupying or annexing attractive slices of Swiss territory—and pushing the Bernese back to their own turf—the French set up a so-called Helvetian Republic. The Swiss abhorred its artificial, centralized structure. Three years of anarchy were put to an end by Napoleon, who gave Switzerland a new constitution (1803) based on the old Confederation, plus six new cantons including Vaud. He also imposed a heavy military levy on the Swiss and took conscripts with him to foreign fields: 8,000 Swiss died covering the emperor's retreat from Moscow.

Neutral but Caring

With the Congress of Vienna (1815) Switzerland's "perpetual neutrality" was restored. Geneva, Neuchâtel and the Valais joined the Confederation, filling out the present-day boundaries of the country. A new constitution of 1848 mapped out the grass-roots democracy still in force, with power shared by local, cantonal and federal authorities.

Switzerland's neutrality faced two harrowing tests in the 20th century—the World Wars. In each case the Swiss army and people were mobilized to defend the frontiers at any cost. In the summer of 1940 it seemed touch-and-go whether Hitler would invade, if only on general principles. The commanding general, Henri Guisan, is considered a great national hero—not for winning a war but for forging an army impressive enough to keep Switzerland out of the war.

Neutrality has propelled Switzerland to a unique position in world affairs. The special role began in 1863, when a businessman from Geneva, Henry Dunant, founded the Red Cross. (Its symbol, a red cross on a white background, is the reverse image of the flag of Switzerland.) The country has given asylum to political exiles of nearly all beliefs, from Lenin to Solzhenytsin. The League of Nations was born in Geneva, now the European headquarters of the United Nations. But Switzerland chose not to join the U.N. itself, for fear of prejudicing national neutrality.

Today, this small country stands as a model of democracy, stability and prosperity for much of the world. The Swiss now face the challenge of striking a balance between commercial interests and moral considerations, between disengagement and humanitarian principles, trying to preserve their unique assets while finding their role in the 20th century.

Red and white national flag flies through the air as twirler opens a traditional Swiss wrestling meet.

Where to Go

Although it's hemmed in by two mountain chains, the Jura and the Alps, French-speaking Switzerland has plenty of wide-open spaces. An hour's trip in any direction runs through glorious scenic contrasts: snow-topped peaks, semi-tropical flower gardens, timberlands and pastures, harsh gorges and dreamy lakes. But don't underestimate the towns and villages, full of charm and tradition.

Getting around is easy. You can drive on well-kept roads or use first-class public transport. Trains are fast and fantastically

punctual. Efficient bus services fill out the map. Within the cities trolley-buses and buses go everywhere swiftly. In the mountains cable-cars and funiculars, Swiss specialities, take you into the wild blue yonder. (You can walk or ski back down if you prefer.)

For convenience, French-speaking Switzerland has been divided here into segments

High above earthly cares, skiers and sightseers in cable cars float across rugged Swiss mountains. Skyline: Valais and Bernese Alps.

which don't always coincide with the cantonal boundaries. We've included a couple of daring forays across the language barrier to German-speaking Switzerland. And other excursions across the easygoing national frontier to neighbouring France.

To begin with, at the westernmost tip of Switzerland, the nation's most international city.

Geneva
Pop. 155,000

This gracious city of history and the arts, glittering shops and waterfront parks is big enough to have everything you're looking for, yet small enough to cope with. Diplomats and international functionaries hang on fiercely when threatened with a transfer. After all, Geneva has that lake, those mountains, that mild climate... and is surrounded on three sides by French cooking.

Geneva's location has been considered crucial ever since 58 B.C., when Julius Caesar and his legions rolled in. They destroyed the ancient bridge across the Rhone, right in the centre of the town, to bar Helvetian tribesmen from migrating to the south of France. Many another ruler has coveted Geneva and its strategic

traffic and trade. The city has been variously controlled by the kings of Burgundy, the Holy Roman Emperor, the dukes of Savoy and, briefly, Napoleon.

In the most memorable battle for Geneva, several thousand mercenaries under the Savoyard flag attacked in 1602. They scaled the town wall at night, but the citizens, armed with anything from pikes to stewpots, sent them flying. Every December 12, Geneva celebrates L'Escalade (scaling of the walls) with a solemn but triumphant torchlight parade.

Perhaps the most improbable ruler in the town's history was the French theologian John Calvin, who made Geneva a great Protestant centre. In 1541, the citizens invited him to serve as their spiritual leader. Life became severe and dour, but Protestant refugees and pilgrims poured into the town. Today tolerance reigns. Geneva, headquarters of the World Council of Churches, is well supplied with Protestant, Catholic and Orthodox churches, plus a synagogue and a mosque.

For an overall survey of Geneva, take one of the multilingual coach tours which operate all year round. From mid-March to the end of October

excursion companies schedule boat tours every day, ranging from a half-hour look around the port to a 2½-hour survey of lakefront castles, mansions and parks.

Walking through Geneva

A logical start for a stroll is the main railway station, the Gare de Cornavin. From here it's a five-minute walk down Rue du Mont-Blanc to the lakeside— that is, if you can stay aloof from the shops and cafés lying in ambush along the way.

The tallest monument in Geneva, visible from many parts of town, is as impermanent as a summer shower. It is, in fact, a jet of water prosaically named the **Jet d'Eau.** When the wind is still, this fireman's dream is turned on, pumping lake water straight up at 500 litres per second to the height of a 40-storey building. Something like this fountain has been a trademark of Geneva's harbour for nearly a century, though the modern model is far more powerful—and more expensive to run.

The Mont-Blanc bridge is the longest and busiest one connecting the two halves of Geneva. Here you can sense a drastic change in the waterway, narrowing from a placid lake to become a surging river. The Rhone River, born high in the Alps, flows the length of Lake Geneva until this spot, where the lake ends and the mighty river resumes its rush toward the Mediterranean.

Notice the small wooded island (man-made in the 16th century) just west of the Mont-Blanc bridge. The contem-

plative statue honours a distinguished Genevan, the philosopher Jean-Jacques Rousseau (1712–78). Behind his back is a sanctuary for swans and ducks. At feeding time all the neighbouring pigeons swoop in without invitation.

A larger island, down-river, bears the laconic name of **l'Ile** (the island). Part of an ancient watch-tower has been preserved; a plaque quotes the historian Caesar on his visit to Geneva.

Once across the river you can

Glass façade of a modern building reflects on Geneva's Rue du Rhône.

wander up the Rue de la Corraterie, an elegant 19th-century shopping street, to the Place Neuve. Three extremely formal buildings face this spacious square: the **Grand Théâtre** (a smaller version of the Paris opera house), the Conservatoire de Musique, and the **Musée Rath**, which presents temporary art exhibits.

Behind iron gates, in the park facing Place Neuve, stands the imposing **Reformation Monument.** A long stone wall is engraved with religious texts in several languages (including 16th-century English). The major sculptural group portrays Calvin and three of his associates: the French reformers Théodore de Bèze and Guillaume Farel, and the Scottish preacher John Knox. Opposite the monument is the main building of the University of Geneva, a descendant of Calvin's theological academy.

Uphill from here is Geneva's **old town,** a well-preserved village of twisting streets, historic mansions and simple fountains lavishly embellished with flowers. Because of the strategic hilltop location, this was the area first fortified by the Romans, as you'll see from restored portions of the ancient city walls.

The highest point of the old town has been a place of worship since pagan days. The present **Cathédrale St-Pierre** (St. Peter's Cathedral) was begun in the 12th century in Romanesque style but evolved into Gothic innovation. In the 18th century the façade was remodelled, and classical columns, still controversial, were tacked on.

Of course, when it was built the cathedral was a Catholic church. Its spontaneous conversion to Protestantism occurred on Sunday, August 8, 1535, when a devout mob of Reformation enthusiasts swept into the temple and resident Catholic priests fled. Calvin preached in St-Pierre (stripped of statues, relics and images of saints) for more than 20 years.

The interior of the cathedral has recently been torn apart in a major reconstruction programme. Until the dust settles, the only peaceful places are the Flamboyant Gothic Chapel of the Maccabees (separate entrance from outside the cathedral, south side) and the belfry. You can climb to the top

Monumental figures of the Reformation loom above pensive pilgrims.

24

of the north tower, amidst the carillon bells, for a top-flight **panorama** of Geneva and vicinity.

This may include the rugged Jura mountains to the north and west and Mount Salève and even Mont-Blanc—if you're lucky—in France (see pp. 30–31).

A few steps from the cathedral, at Place de la Taconnerie, you can visit the modest chapel in which John Knox preached to English-language adherents of the new faith. The church, called the Auditoire de Calvin, was submitted to a brighter-than-new restoration programme in 1959.

Under the arcades of a building called the **Arsenal,** partly camouflaged behind flowerpots, cannon from the 17th and 18th centuries are symbolically deployed. Modern mosaics give an impression of medieval Geneva.

Geneva's **Hôtel de Ville** (town hall), across the street from the Arsenal, has an elegant Renaissance courtyard. A ramp, not a staircase, runs upstairs; visiting dignitaries could be driven all the way to their meetings at the summit. The first of the Geneva conventions on the humane treatment of prisoners-of-war was concluded in the town hall in 1864.

Soon afterwards, an international dispute growing out of the American Civil War was settled here. The historic chamber is now called, somewhat startlingly, the Salle de l'Alabama—after a Confederate warship of the same name.

The street running past the town hall turns into picturesque **Grand-Rue,** lined with buildings dating from the 15th to the 18th centuries. A plaque on the front of No. 40 indicates the house where Jean-Jacques Rousseau was born.

Back around the corner from the Hôtel de Ville, on a bluff overlooking the Promenade des Bastions, you can relax in a tree-shaded park called La Treille (the Trellis). Originally a vineyard, now a municipal park, it features what Genevans proudly call the longest park bench in the world.

International City

The elegant Quai Wilson, along the right bank of the lake, honours the 20th-century American president who profoundly affected Geneva's destiny. The city had long been a centre of book-publishing, watch-making, banking… as well as intellectual and humanitarian activities. Woodrow Wilson made it the world headquarters of diplomacy. Founding the League of Nations, he nominated Geneva as its site.

In the 60 years since that big decision, countless new international organizations and agencies have been created, and most of them seem to have set up shop in the congenial surroundings of the League's old home town. They are as diverse as the International Telecommunications Union, the International Labour Office (ILO), the General Agreement on Tariffs and Trade (GATT) and the little-heard-of World Organization for the Protection of Intellectual Property.

The spacious **Palais des Nations** was the headquarters of the League of Nations. Designed by an international committee of architects, it opened for business in 1937, when war clouds already overshadowed the League's good intentions. After World War II had run its course, the new United Nations took over the building for its European headquarters. As U.N. activities and personnel rolls inexorably multiplied, the building was further expanded, rapidly eclipsing the Palais de Versailles in acreage.

The U.N. runs half-hour guided tours. If the diplomatic heavyweights don't happen to be tussling over a treaty in closed session, you'll be taken to visit historic conference halls. You may have reservations about the architectural merit of the building, but you'll certainly like the delegates' view of the lake and the Alps.

Parks and Gardens

Geneva is rightly proud of its rich, roomy parks with their fountains, sculptures, bandstands and cafés. The highlights:

Jardin Anglais (English Garden), on the left bank, is lush and inviting. It's best known for the **flower clock**—a huge dial made up of thousands of flowers and plants changed seasonally.

Parc de la Grange features a truly sensational rose garden. Elsewhere in the park the remains of an ancient Roman villa were excavated, proving again that the Romans had good taste in real estate. **Parc des Eaux Vives,** adjoining the Grange, is beautifully landscaped.

Across the lake you'll find **Parc Mon Repos** and, next to it, **Perle du Lac** park which includes a distinguished restaurant. Inland, the **Jardin Botanique** (botanical garden) mixes beauty and erudition. **27**

And in a mini-park on the right bank, on the Quai du Mont-Blanc, Geneva's most bizarre monument: the **tomb of the Duke of Brunswick** (1804–73). Having spent his last few years in exile in Geneva, the eccentric gentleman bequeathed the city many a worthwhile project.

Museums of Geneva

Musée d'Art et d'Histoire. Geneva's biggest and richest museum covers a lot of ground, from prehistory to modern art. An outstanding archaeological collection features local and faraway discoveries over many centuries. The most highly prized item is an altarpiece painted for St. Peter's Cathedral by Conrad Witz in 1444. Called *The Miracle of the Fishes*, it shows the Geneva countryside—the first time a European painter depicted a non-fictional background.

Musée Ariana. In a marble-columned palace surrounded by parkland, the art of ceramics unfolds from medieval Spanish pottery to modern porcelain. The park, the museum and much of the collection were donated to Geneva by a 19th century philanthropist, Gustave Revilliod, who named the institution after his mother.

Musée de l'Horlogerie. Classic clocks tick and chime in an 18th-century mansion, Villa de Malagnou. Immensely delicate enamelled watches were a Genevan speciality.

Petit Palais. Four floors of a small palace are packed with impressionist and post-impressionist works of varying quality. Renoir and Picasso are there, but the emphasis is on lesser-known artists of the era.

Musée d'Instruments Anciens de Musique. Fritz Ernst, who collected these 300 historic musical instruments, plays some of them for visitors. He calls it the only living museum in the world. (Check unusual opening hours.)

Geneva has about a dozen more museums, including a pair devoted to the men who made the city a great 18th-century intellectual centre—Rousseau and Voltaire. In spite of their vastly differing views and styles, both authors at one time had their works banned by Geneva's ultra-righteous censor.

Note: Museum visiting hours tend to change from time to time, so it's best to consult the lists in the tourist office before setting out. Most museums, though, are open from 10 a.m. to noon and from 2 to 5 or 6 p.m. and closed on Mondays.

28

Carouge

Though it seems like an extension of Geneva, Carouge is a separate municipality on the south bank of the Arve River with its very own history and character. It was founded in the late 18th century by—of all unlikely powers—the King of Sardinia, who also happened to be the Duke of Savoy. In those days titles and crowns were passed around like any other family heirlooms.

The Sardinians' imperial

Assessing a rare antique, Geneva expert holds it with loving hands.

plan for Carouge was to create a serious rival to Geneva. Most of the project stayed on the drawing board, but there's no mistaking the foreignness of the town's fountains and squares, wrought-iron street-lamps and faded town-houses.

Genevans like to go to Carouge for the round-the-clock bohemian atmosphere—theatre and art and lively bars and restaurants. A colourful street market is held on Wednesday and Saturday mornings.

Foreign Affairs

Geneva is a peninsula jutting into France, so crossing the border is as commonplace as crossing town. Here are two spots the Genevans often visit on the foreign side of the rather easy-going frontier.

The Salève. This mountain is such a familiar bit of scenery for Genevans that it might as

Alpine scenes and other paintings for sale at a quaint Geneva shop.

well be a local monument. On weekends the strangely tilted cliff-face swarms with local mountain-climbers. Other intrepid sportsmen drive to the top (4,525 ft.) to practise the breathtaking art of hang-gliding. The view from the summit is superb.

Divonne. In this overgrown French village, 18 kilometres north of Geneva, you can restore your health or (much less likely) your fortune. The two principal attractions are the thermal baths and the gambling casino. Big money changes hands around the roulette, blackjack, baccarat and craps tables in an old-fashioned continental atmosphere. In summer Divonne widens its horizons with horse-racing, golf, sailing and a distinguished chamber-music festival.

Chamonix

On a very clear day you can see three-mile-high **Mont-Blanc** from the centre of Geneva, but for a close-up of Europe's highest summit you have to cross the border into France. This very popular all-day excursion takes two hours by coach from Geneva. Or you can do it yourself by car or train.

As the Matterhorn has brought fame to Zermatt, so Mont-Blanc casts its shadow and spell over the town of Chamonix. This top European winter-sports centre has the air of an Alaskan gold-rush town, with improvised architectural styles plopped together wherever a level space could be found. But the appearance of the town itself is all very secondary to the overwhelming beauty of the encircling Alps.

From Chamonix you can take one of the world's highest cable-cars above pines, stone and snow to the blinding white summit of the **Aiguille du Midi** at an altitude of 12,600 feet. At the top end of this breathtaking journey you walk across a footbridge spanning a crevasse whose depths may be invisible in snow and mist and climb to an observation station. What you see from the Aiguille du Midi depends on the weather—a head-on portrait of Mont-Blanc and unforgettable panoramas over the glacier, or perhaps nothing more than snowflakes filling a stormy sky.

Another excursion from Chamonix is by funicular to the **Mer de Glace** ("sea of ice"), where you can enter an ice-grotto and try walking around on the glacier. The trip is now very comfortable. Before the railway was built, 300 mules were employed to transport tourists to the glacier.

The Lake of Geneva

Geneva's lake—and Lausanne's, Montreux's and Evian's—is really named Léman. It has won the hearts of poets, artists, composers... and geographers and statisticians.

The largest in the Alps, about two thirds of it belongs to Switzerland, one-third to France. The lake is almost 45 miles long and up to $8^1/_2$ miles wide, for a total area of nearly 225 square miles.

On this mini-sea, five-foot waves can spring up suddenly. Pleasure boaters are always on the alert for perilous winds.

But much of the time it's clear sailing: a pageant of brightly striped spinnakers billowing under a pale sky crosshatched with jet-trails; white lake-steamers manœuvering among motorboats, canoes, windsurfers and self-confident swans and ducks. Ashore, holidaymakers and locals politely vie for seats under the red parasols of outdoor cafés, where tiny glasses are filled and refilled with the local white wine—an appropriate salute to the glorious convergence here of mountains, lake and sky.

Lakeside cafés and parks offer one perspective on the Lake of Geneva and the ever-present Alps beyond. For another point of view, relax aboard an excursion boat sweeping by sunny vineyards, patrician houses and old stone villages (see p. 106). Or take the corniche road high above the lake and see how the vineyards, laid out in disciplined rows, are terraced all the way down to the gently curving shore. You can even walk all the way around the lake—given a week or two.

However you do it, try to see as many facets as possible of this unforgettable mountain lake. Even in mist and rain—

Sailing Close to the Wind

The Swiss worry about their wind currents the way the French worry about their livers. If the wind blows from the north, a cold *bise*, it's the subject of knowing conversation all day. If it's a dry, warm *föhn*, they say, you can expect headaches, stress and sometimes vertigo.

Down at the lakes, charts warn inexperienced sailors to watch for legendary local winds that might blow no good. On the Lake of Geneva, winds have names like Joran, Vent Blanc, Fraidieu, Vaudaire and Séchard. The most tempestuous of all is the French-based Bornan, which comes on at a hurricane-like 60 to 85 miles an hour.

not exactly a novelty in winter—the special lure of the Lake of Geneva is undeniable.

For reasons of organization, our coverage of the lake shore's most interesting towns and landmarks begins on the eastern edge of Geneva and continues clockwise almost full circle.

La Côte

Coppet. This pleasant village of thick-walled stone houses evokes the image of Europe's 19th-century superwoman, Germaine Necker, better known as Mme de Staël. Her father, the Genevan banker Jacques Necker, bought the **château** of Coppet in 1784. A white marble statue of the gentleman, clad in a toga, stands in the entrance hall.

But the point of the mansion, which is open for guided tours, is the brilliant Mme de Staël. Her portraits and memorabilia are scattered through rooms furnished in Louis XVI and Directoire style. When Napoleon exiled her from Paris, she took her intellectual salon, including the leading lights of French romanticism, along to Coppet. As one of her circle, the aristocratic philosopher Charles-Victor de Bonstetten observed: "More wit is dispensed at Coppet in one day than in the rest of the world in a year."

The château is closed on Mondays and during the winter.

Nyon. While the château of Coppet evolved into a purely residential building, the five-towered **castle** of Nyon was designed and used as a military bastion by the Savoy family. Construction began in the 12th century. In the 16th century the fortress was overpowered by troops from Berne, who then controlled the Canton of Vaud for the next 250 years. The château houses local government offices, museums and, on the top floor, a prison (still in use) with a painfully beautiful view of the freedom outside—the Lake of Geneva and the Alps.

Julius Caesar established an army outpost here, and the Romans are well remembered in the château's history museum, which has rooms full of ancient amphoras and statuary. Upstairs a separate museum is devoted to examples of the porcelain produced in Nyon in the late 18th and early 19th centuries and now fiercely coveted by collectors.

Another memento of the Romans: two and a half Corinthian columns, discovered under a nearby street, which have been effectively installed on the edge of a bluff at the end of the **Promenade des Vieilles Murailles** ("old walls walk"). Spread out below is a neatly gardened park and a port for both pleasure-craft and fishing boats. You may find the local anglers using a public fountain to keep a few dozen big perch alive until market time.

The fishing industry, along with historic and scientific aspects of the lake, are covered in Le Musée du Léman, a waterfront museum.

The old centre of Nyon, around the château, is a pleasure to explore: an 11th-century tower, a 12th-century church, and dozens of exemplary houses from the 15th to 19th centuries.

Rolle. Most castles were built on hilltops for strategic reasons, but the 13th-century château of Rolle, halfway between Geneva and Lausanne, is right on the lakefront. It has seen its share of fighting. The Bernese burned it twice in the 16th century.

Near the castle are pleasant lakefront promenades. Just offshore is a singular sight: a lonely artificial island. Tall trees overshadow an obelisk dedicated to Rolle's most revered citizen, Frédéric-César de La Harpe (1754–1838), known as the father of the independence of the Canton of Vaud. At the Congress of Vienna (1814–15) he was instrumental in obtaining guarantees of the neutrality of Switzerland and the independence of Vaud and several other cantons. In an earlier career, La Harpe served as tutor to Tsar Alexander I of Russia.

Saint-Prex. In this unselfconsciously quaint medieval market town, barns and shops stand among distinguished mansions. A heavy clock tower dated 1234 surmounts the landward side of the short main street leading to the lake.

Morges. When it's tulip time in Morges you know that winter has finally been chased from the shores of the Lake of Geneva. Every April and May the Morges Tulip Festival stars more than 100 varieties of tulips—perhaps 300,000 flowers in all.

Before the railway was built, Morges had been an important port for lake freighters. It's still a nautical centre, but the boats are dinghies and yachts moored in Morges' marina by weekend sailors who live all along the coast.

Commanding the waterfront is an imposing square **château** built in the 13th century. The

LAKE OF GENEVA

castle and the town itself were founded by Prince Louis of Savoy as a power base to rival the prince-bishop of Lausanne. Since the 19th century, parts of the building have been used as a military arsenal. In 1871 an ammunition explosion killed a score of people and broke windows as far away as Thonon, on the French side of the lake. The château now encloses the **Vaud Military Museum,** with historical costumes, battle-flags and weapons and more toy soldiers than you've ever seen—8,000 little lead figurines deployed to re-create ancient and modern battles.

Another local museum, **Musée Alexis Forel,** is a 16th-century mansion filled with valuable antique furniture and works of art.

A footnote for music-lovers. The Polish composer and statesman Ignace Paderewski lived in Morges for some years. And Igor Stravinsky composed *L'Histoire du Soldat,* in col-

The final touch and everything is ready for sailing regatta at Morges.

laboration with the Swiss author C.-F. Ramuz, in Morges in 1918.

Saint-Sulpice. The waterfront park of this quiet village is furnished with striking modern statues. There are gratifying views of the vineyards, the lake and the mountains across the way, and even an unexpected sidelong glimpse of Lausanne a few miles down the coast.

But the main reason for visiting Saint-Sulpice is a few yards inland: a touching primitive **Romanesque church.** Topped by a heavy square belfry, it was built in the 11th or 12th-century as part of a Benedictine monastery. In the 15th century the nave collapsed but the choir and transept stand by themselves as a pleasing and important architectural monument. **37**

Lausanne

Pop. 135.000

If anything's missing in Lausanne, it may be the generation gap. Cheerful coexistence links the teenager on a skateboard with the retired tycoon in a wheelchair. Old and young, tourist and native share a sense of well-being in this prosperous business, government and university centre. Something's always going on—an international music festival or an industrial exhibition or just a street-corner jazz recital.

Lausanne's mile-long lakefront, with parks and gardens, cafés and restaurants, is the liveliest, loveliest place in town when the weather's fair. More than 1,400 pleasure boats, including oceanworthy yachts, are moored in two local marinas. This is also the home port of a veritable Swiss navy of excursion ships. Watch a big white steamboat gently nudge against the wharf, letting off hordes of partying passengers. Or you can get into the swim by renting a rowing boat or a pedalo.

This part of town, called **Ouchy** (pronounced oo-shee), is not for serious sightseeing, but in your wanderings you may sight two structures of apparent importance. Right at the

port, the Château d'Ouchy is a real medieval castle but it was almost totally rebuilt in the 19th century and is now a hotel. If you walk eastward to the end of the landscaped waterfront promenade, you'll be startled to see the ruins of a medieval tower. Actually it's a counterfeit, built in 1823 as a bit of a joke between local businessmen.

From Ouchy to the centre of Lausanne is too long and steep a walk to appeal to most tourists. An unusual, efficient way of going up is the grandly named Métro, a wide-bodied rack-railway train that makes the ascent in six minutes. Old-

timers still call the Métro "La Ficelle" (the string) after the original funicular built a century ago. The right-of-way alongside the track is landscaped with flowers and blooming trees. At the fourth (last) stop, called Centre Ville, take the lift up to the level of Lausanne's main traffic intersection, **Place St-François.**

This hectic square, a conglomeration of banks, shops and trolleybus stops, used to be the site of a Franciscan monastery. All that's left, on an island of peace in the middle of all this activity is the 13th-century church of **St-François.** Inside and out it's a sober work of architecture except for the 15th-century clock-tower with four turrets and a slim spire. Since 1536 it has been a Protestant church.

One of Lausanne's smartest shopping streets, the cobbled **Rue de Bourg,** wanders steeply upward from Place St-François, mostly traffic-free. If you continue climbing on Rue Caroline you'll come upon an open expanse with a first-class view of the towers of the cathedral. To get there, cross the Bessières bridge.

Only the ferry's in a hurry on a lazy day in Lausanne's port, Ouchy.

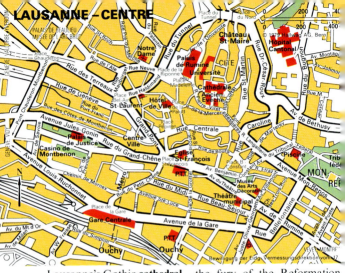

Lausanne's Gothic **cathedral** is one of the last places in the world preserving the tradition of the night watch. The night hours (10 p.m. to 2 a.m.) are called out by a watchman surveying the city from his tower.

Construction began in the 12th century. The cathedral was consecrated in 1275 at a ceremony attended by Pope Gregory X, seven cardinals, five archbishops, 17 bishops and King Rudolph of the incipient Habsburg empire.

Among remarkable 13th-century survivals in this important cathedral are a rare set of choir stalls and, almost miraculously, a **rose window.** In the fury of the Reformation almost all of the cathedral's stained-glass windows were shattered, but most of the elements of this admirable squared-circle survived. Restoration work was started in the 19th century by that eminent fixer-up of old monuments (Notre-Dame de Paris, Carcassonne) Eugène Viollet-le-Duc.

Alongside the cathedral, another historic building, the former episcopal palace, is now the **Musée Historique de l'Ancien Evêché.** Archaeological details of the town and the cathedral are on view, along with the statues of prophets

40

and apostles which originally surrounded the south portal in the early 13th century. They have survived erosion and wear because they were painted.

Between the cathedral and the 15th-century **Château St-Maire,** now headquarters of the Vaud cantonal government, is **La Cité,** a neighbourhood

Hirsute troubadour entertains the passing crowds in Rue de Bourg.

Headless Hero
Set against the south façade of the château is a monument to Major Jean-Daniel Abraham Davel (1670–1723), who challenged the canton's Bernese rulers to grant independence to Vaud. He recruited 600 soldiers and marched on Lausanne with a manifesto. He was arrested and promptly executed—decapitated in Vidy.

Unfortunately, Major Davel was 80 years ahead of his time.

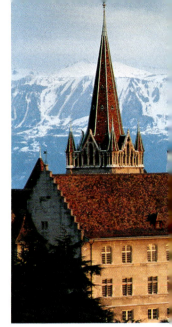

Last rays of winter sun highlight the towers of Lausanne's cathedral.

of university and government buildings and antique shops. See the panorama from the terrace between the château and the building of the Grand Conseil (cantonal legislature)—the best sunsets in town!

Covered staircases lead from the cathedral to **Place de la Palud,** Lausanne's marketplace since medieval times. On Wednesday and Saturday mornings the entire area becomes an irresistible street market—flowers, temptingly arranged vegetables and fruits, country bread and cakes. This does not detract from the dignity of Lausanne's 17th-century **Hôtel de Ville** (city hall), with its arches, capricious clocktower and fierce gargoyles. The fountain in the square portrays Justice as a good-looking woman showing a bit more leg than is usual on these occasions. It is a 20th-century replica of a 16th-century statue.

The Saturday flea market centres on Place de la Riponne, Lausanne's biggest square. As you would expect in an over-developed country, the junk is very high class and nothing is very cheap. But you'll enjoy roaming among the displays of antiques, clothes, jewellery and slightly read books.

Lausanne Museums

Riponne's overblown Palais de Rumine, in "Florentine Renaissance" style from the turn of the present century, is big enough to contain several museums. The **Musée Cantonal des Beaux-Arts** (Fine Arts Museum) is strong on Swiss artists. The archaeological department of the museum

gives pride of place to a 22-carat gold likeness of the Roman emperor Marcus Aurelius (A.D. 121–180) affecting a very contemporary haircut and beard. The 3½-pound bust was discovered at Avenches (see pp. 78, 80).

La Collection d'Art Brut, in a converted château near the Palais de Beaulieu convention centre, is quite possibly the most original, haunting museum in Switzerland. *Art brut* (literally raw art) is sometimes translated as "outsiders' art". Each artist displayed here has *invented* his or her own school of art, and often the implements and medium as well. The results are quite astonishing flights of genius by untrained talents, some of them mentally unbalanced. The psychological history of each artist is posted along with more conventional biographical details (in French only). This 5,000-piece collection was founded by the French artist Jean Dubuffet. **43**

The **Musée Romain de Vidy,** near the site of a 15th-century leper colony at Maladière, displays old Roman statuary and inscriptions unearthed in the surrounding area. Of unusual value is a collection of 72 Roman gold coins that were amassed by a Roman numismatist of the 2nd century A.D.

On the other side of the *autoroute,* near the lakefront, was the original Roman settlement of Lousonna. The layout of the ancient town's centre is clearly visible in the foundations of the

Imagination unleashed: "raw art" on view in Collection d'Art Brut.

buildings in the Vidy archaeo-logical zone. The ruins have been preserved and tidied in Swiss style.

By coincidence, the defini-tive history of Rome was writ-ten in Lausanne. Edward Gib-bon (1737–94) finished his *History of the Decline and Fall of the Roman Empire* during the years he spent as a houseguest around the corner from Place St-François. Like the empire, Gibbon's house has fallen.

Parlez-Vous Suisse?
Your school French will serve you well in Suisse Romande, though local accents and into-nations may sound a bit odd. Some Swiss words differ from the classic French. In many towns, they say *syndic*, for example, instead of *maire* for mayor; *septante*, *huitante* and *nonante* are the usual words in these parts for seventy, eighty and ninety; and you're likely to hear people referring to breakfast as *déjeuner*, the mid-day meal as *dîner* and evening eating as *souper*.

Academics in Neuchâtel are compiling a dictionary of the many local *patois* (unofficial dialects) of French-speaking Switzerland. At last report, they had put together 3,800 pages and were only up to the letter "e".

Vaud Riviera

Sprawling in the sun from the outskirts of Lausanne to the eastern end of the Lake of Geneva, the Vaud Riviera is a land of sophisticated resorts and one-industry villages per-vaded by the musty smell of wine. You never know what to expect around the next turn in the road—a flower garden, a wine press, a chalet or a château. But you'll almost al-ways be surrounded by steep vineyards which produce the heady Lavaux wine.

No matter how you travel the views are superb—by boat looking up at the golden hill-sides; by train right along the coast; by car on the coast road or the panoramic **Route du Vignoble** (route of the vine-yards) or the utilitarian but spec-tacular *autoroute*.

Towns and villages along the way that rate a glance or a stroll:

Lutry. An unspoiled lake-front town with a Gothic church retaining some original Romanesque details, a château built by the Bernese, and a wine industry humming efficiently unseen in cellars beneath the old stone houses. They hold a rousing wine festival here in October.

Epesses. A typical wine-

growing village with old stone houses and narrow, steep streets; noted for its fine white wine.

Saint-Saphorin. A totally delightful old village of flowered lanes with a 16th-century church and an esteemed (and expensive) local wine.

Vevey

Wine and milk-chocolate keep this lakeside town afloat. The biggest building in Vevey, a curved-glass structure in United Nations style, is the world headquarters of Nestlé, the multinational food company. As for wine, the Romans of 2,000 years ago were probably the first to plant grapes on the local hillsides. The importance of wine has been celebrated about once every 25 years since the 18th century in Vevey's Fête des Vignerons (winegrowers' festival), one of Europe's biggest and happiest folk manifestations (last one held in 1977).

The wine pageant and most other events in Vevey centre on the **Grande Place,** the town's disproportionately big square. On any Saturday it becomes a real country market with a rich mixture of essentials and trivialities on sale: home-baked pastries, slightly outdated fashions, the freshest flowers... or a used fireman's helmet. On his way to Italy, Napoleon reviewed his troops in the Grande Place. Many another foreigner has valued Vevey's more peaceful attractions: Dostoevsky, Gogol, Victor Hugo, Saint-Saëns, Paderewski, Wagner.

Between the lake and the railway station, old Vevey is a walkable district of 18th- and 19th-century houses, often flying traditional emblems which identify shops or cafés.

The **Musée du Vieux-Vevey,** in a lakefront château, shows how things have changed since early times. Another local museum, the **Musée Jenisch,** specializes in Swiss painting of the 19th and 20th centuries.

Above the railway line, surrounded by chestnut trees, stands Vevey's oldest church, **St-Martin.** Its 15th-century tower looks like a compromise between a cathedral and a castle. Actually, it once had a spire that was blown over by freak storms.

A rack-railway takes you from Vevey to **Les Pléiades,** a

Pitching in to gather the grapes in the Lavaux region in October.

belvedere more than 4,500 feet above sea level, with views of the lush landscape down to the lake and across to the French Alps. About halfway up is **Blonay,** with a 12th-century château and a nostalgic tourist railway equipped with turn-of-the-century locomotives and passenger carriages. Steam's up every Saturday and Sunday from May to the end of October on the Blonay-Chamby choo-choo.

From vineyards and orchards above Vevey a funicular climbs to another vantage point, **Mont-Pèlerin,** in a region of woods, farms, villas and sweeping vistas.

Montreux

The lake has narrowed, and the mountains ascending steeply behind Montreux shield the town from north winds. A 3-mile **lakeside promenade** exploits this unique hothouse atmosphere: all kinds of flowers thrive here and even palm trees stand firm on this alien shore.

This is a full-time, big-time tourist resort, where large old-fashioned hotels and a few new ones cater to the cosmopolitan visitor's every whim. The service and the view are so special that novelist Vladimir Nabokov chose to live permanently in his Montreux hotel suite.

The old-world look of the

Steam railway enthusiasts attend to smallest details for authenticity on the nostalgic Blonay-Chamby line.

place is deceptive, for something timely always seems to be going on—an international conference or TV awards or the Montreux Jazz Festival. The new casino on the waterfront adds glamour to the scene, even if hard-core gamblers find its wheels of chance soberly provincial.

Up the hill behind the lakeside glitter is the **old town** with its 18th-century stone houses, chalets, wrought-iron balconies, antique and artisan shops, galleries and huge barns. At the top is the **Temple St-Vincent,** now a Protestant church. A recent renovation successfully melded the 12th- and 15th-century architecture with daringly modern stained-glass windows.

Montreux is a springboard for train trips to ski resorts as famous as Gstaad. Another mountain railway goes up to **Caux,** a balcony over Lake Geneva, and on to **Rochers-de-Naye,** a 6,700-foot summit with an all-round spectacular view and a nearby alpine garden with hundreds of varieties of delicate mountain flowers that bloom in early summer. **49**

Château de Chillon

Switzerland's best-known castle, Chillon is a moody feudal fortress which has known battles and torture, feasts and romance. Its turrets and towers have survived centuries of upheavals and even today they survive the tremor and roar of express trains hurtling past the door. It could have been worse. The 19th-century railway builders wanted to tear down the château and use the historic stones to prop up their right-of-way.

Some fortifications must have been right on this spot since ancient times: the great rock of Chillon, projecting